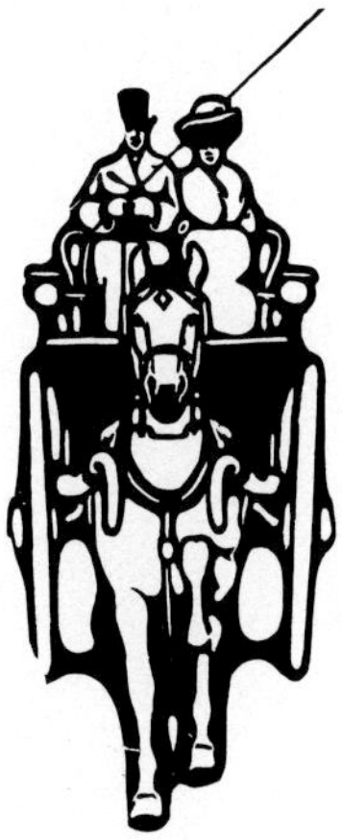

KIV

ICE

SHIELDS
NEWCASTLE
3
OMNIBU
EVERY
HOU

TALLY HO!

POST
CHAISE

ICE

COAL
COAL

COAL

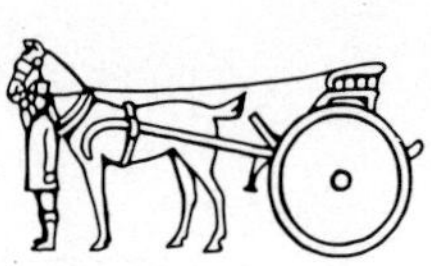

GOODS CAREFULLY REMOVED
ROAD
RAIL
OR
SEA
TO ALL PARTS

CITY OMNIBUS LINE

OMNIBUS LINE.

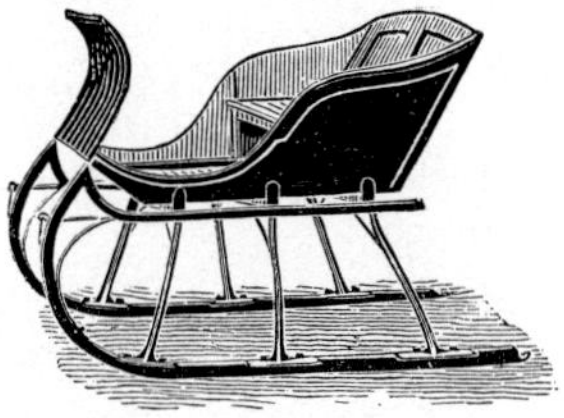

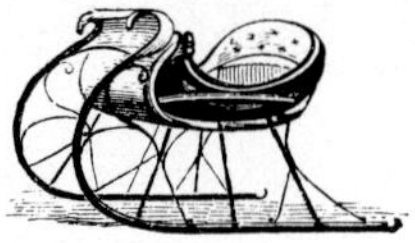

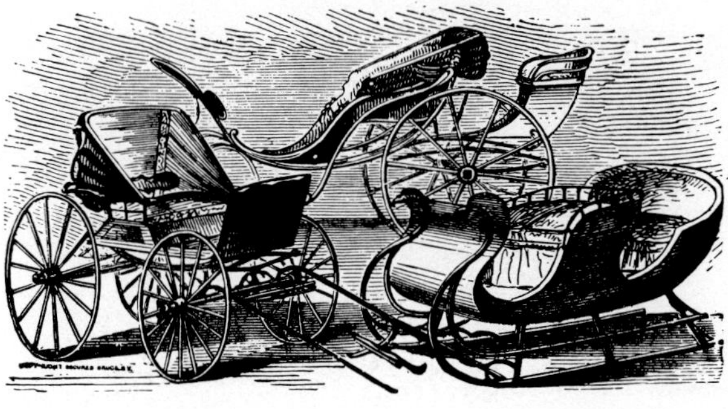

CAMP & PRYTANIA
26
NEW ORLEANS

THE TROLLEY SOAP
JOS. S. & THOS. ELKINTON.

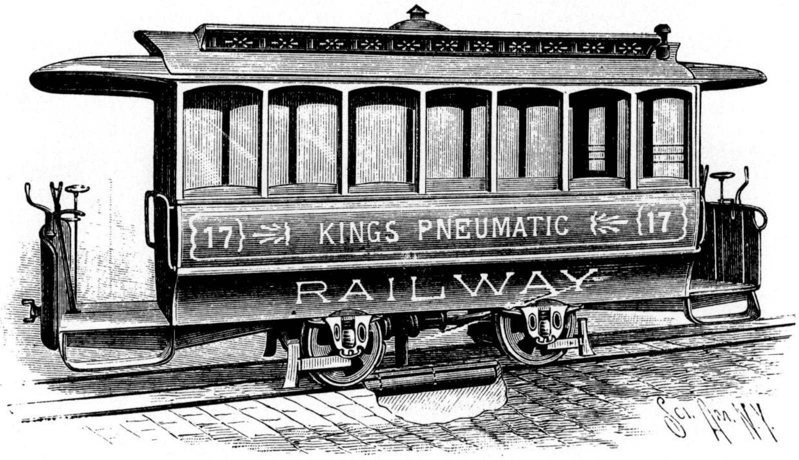
17
KINGS PNEUMATIC
17
RAILWAY

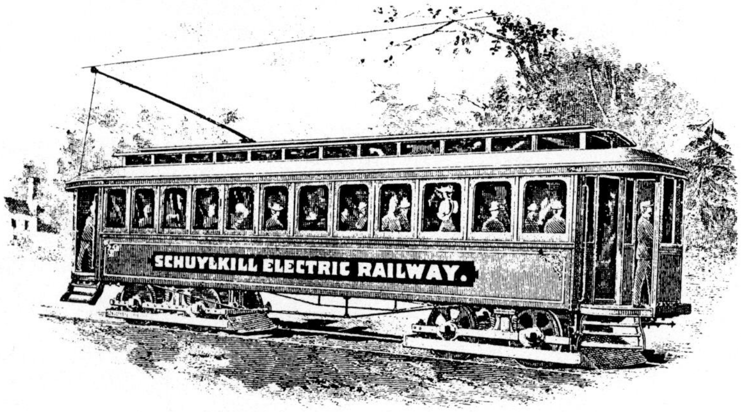
SCHUYLKILL ELECTRIC RAILWAY.

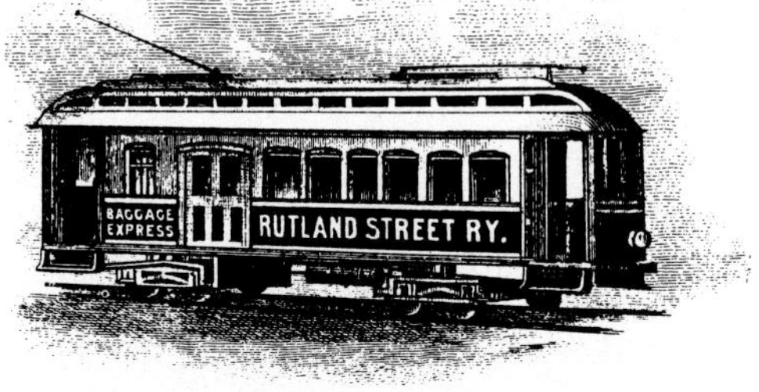
BAGGAGE EXPRESS
RUTLAND STREET RY.

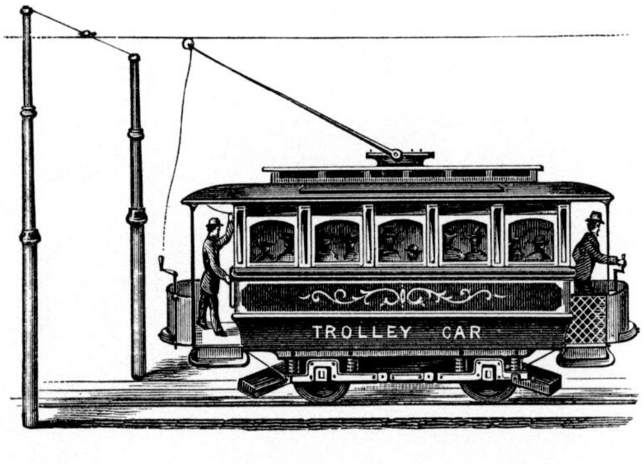
TROLLEY CAR

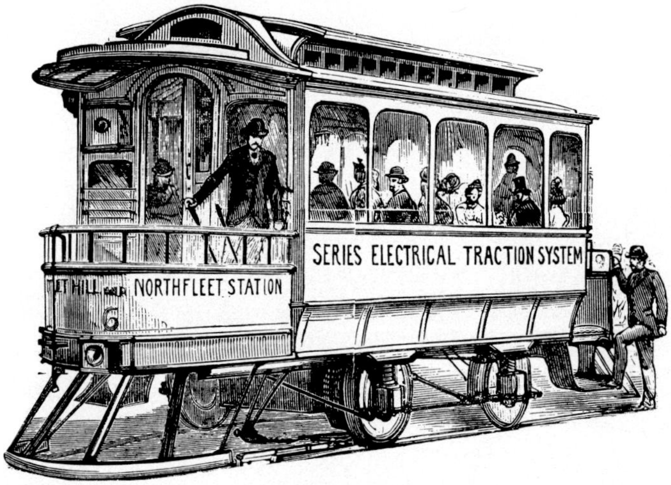
SERIES ELECTRICAL TRACTION SYSTEM
NORTHFLEET STATION

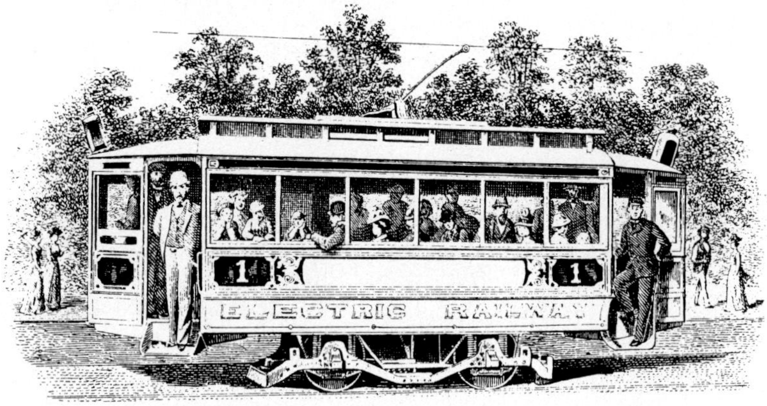
1
ELECTRIC RAILWAY
1

10

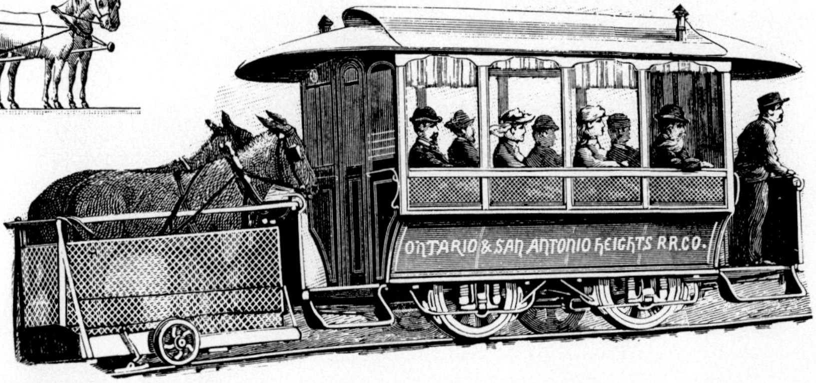
ONTARIO & SAN ANTONIO HEIGHTS R.R.CO.

Metropolitan R. R. Co.

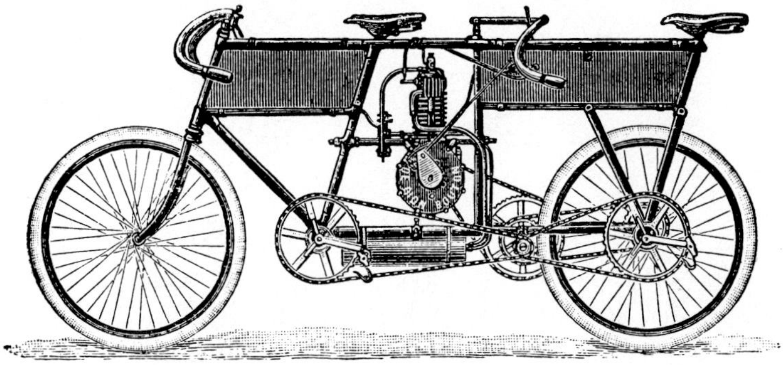

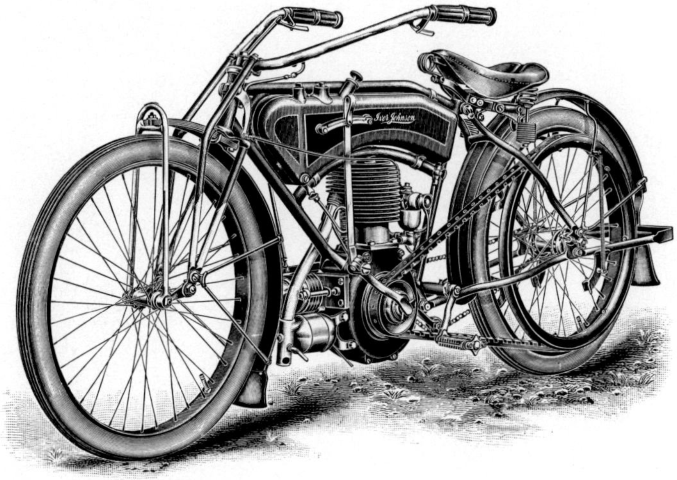

100

EXPRESS

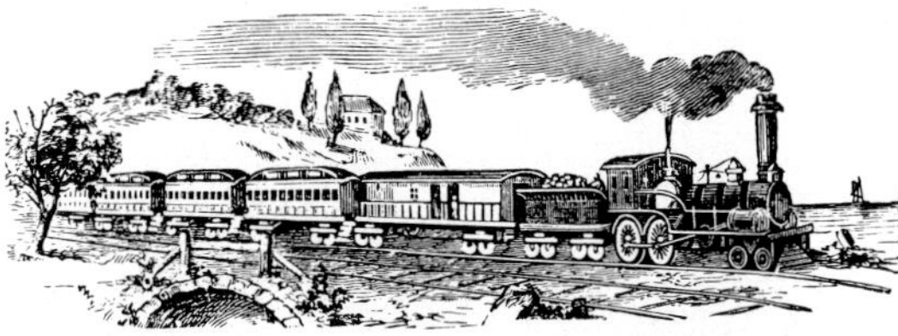

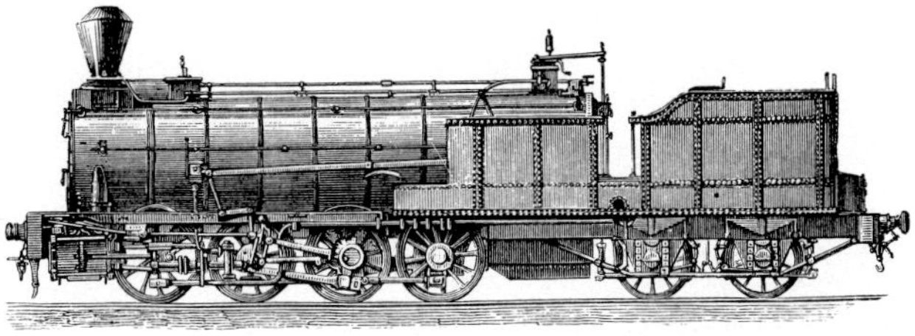

21
CHICAGO
ROCK ISLAND & PACIFIC
ROCKY MOUNTAIN LIMITED
ROCKY MOUNTAIN LIMITED
21

270

B.L.E

SINN

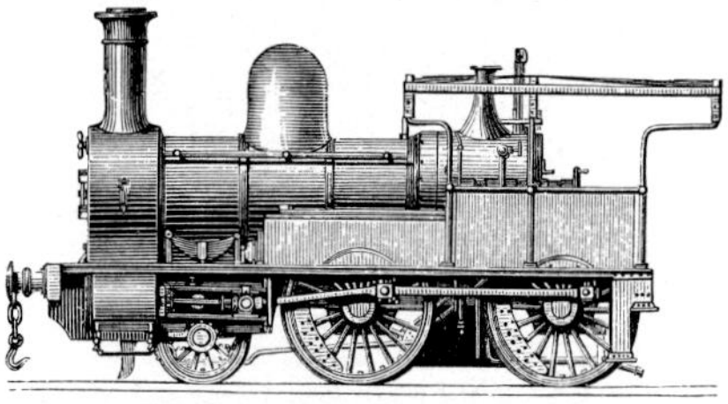

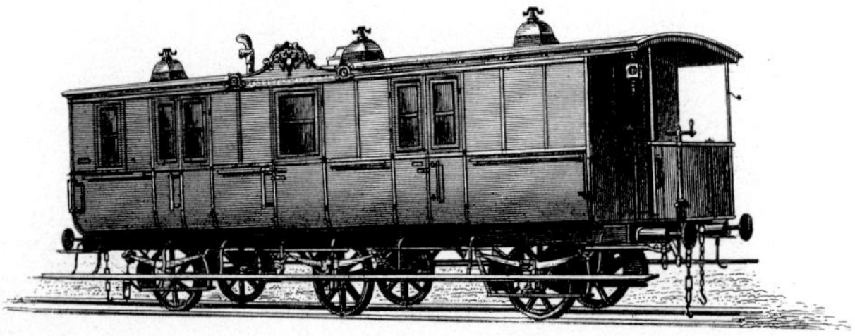

US MAIL
BAGGAGE

USM
EXPRESS

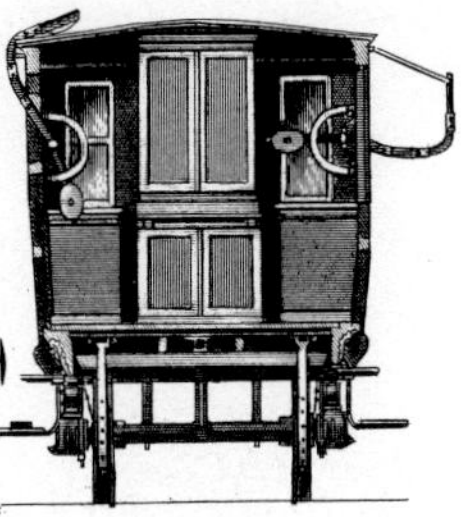

HINKLEY

C.WRIGHT.N.Y.

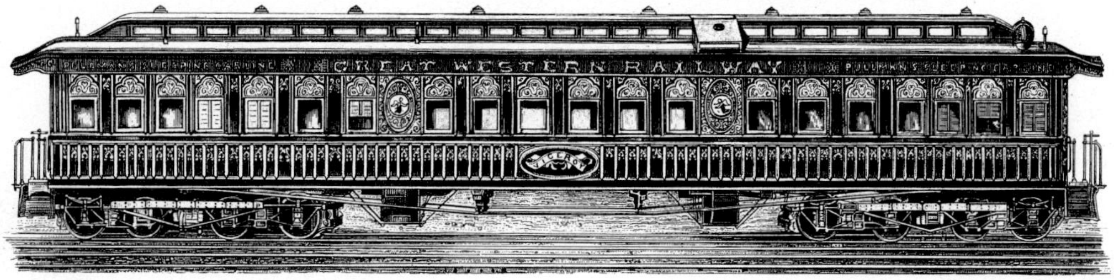
GREAT WESTERN RAILWAY

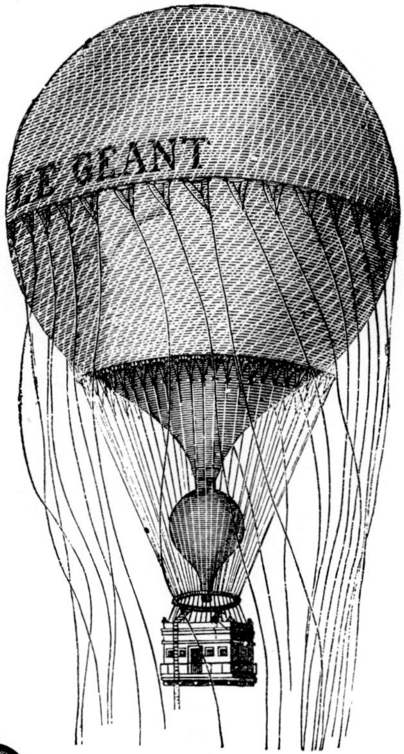
LE GEANT

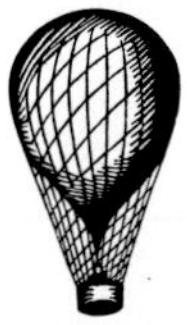

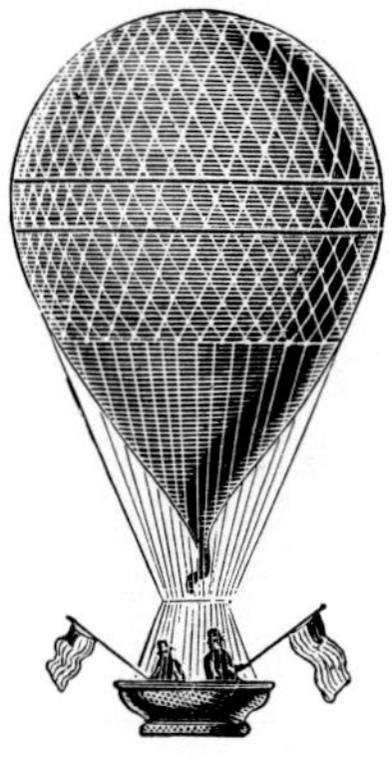

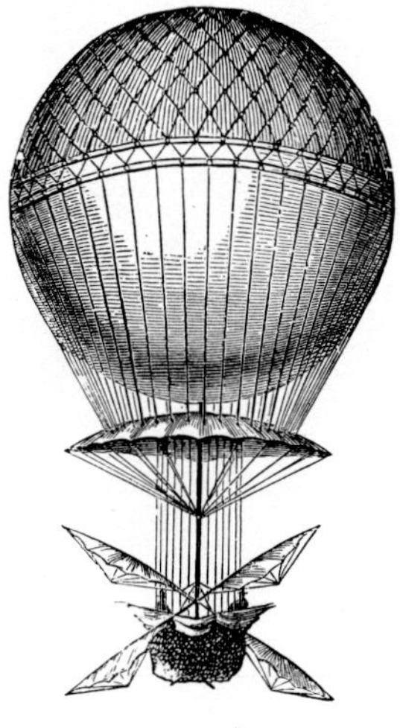

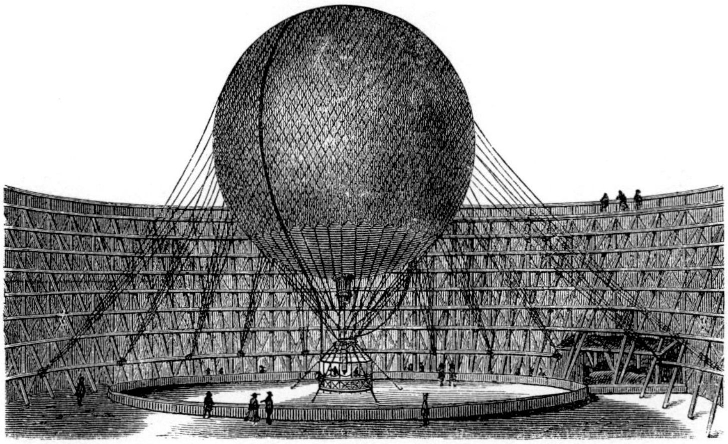

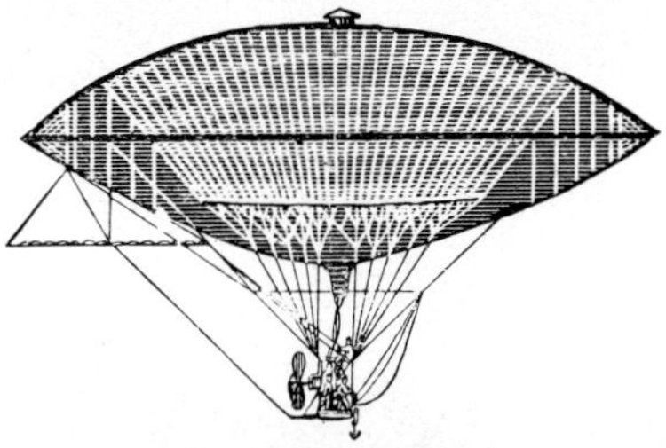
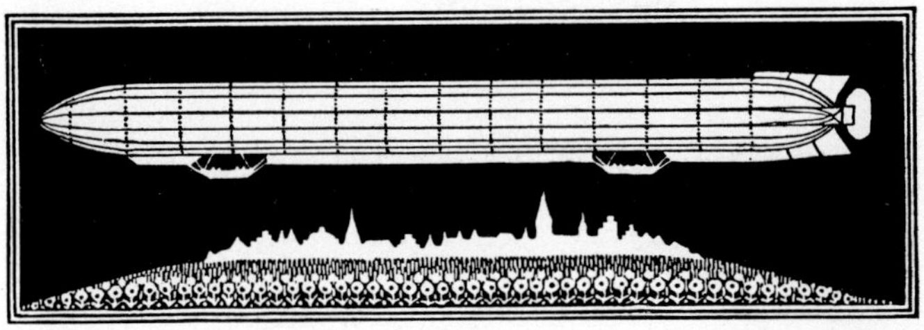

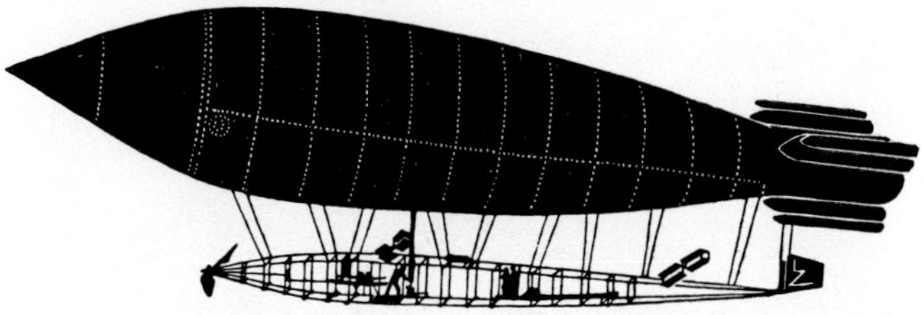
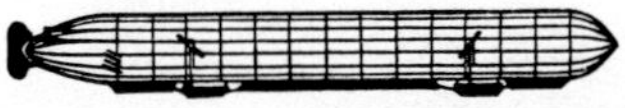
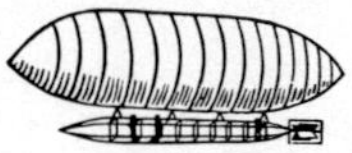
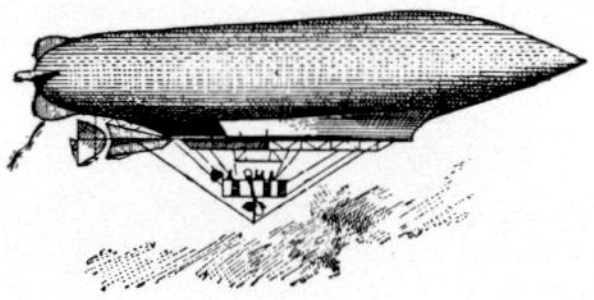
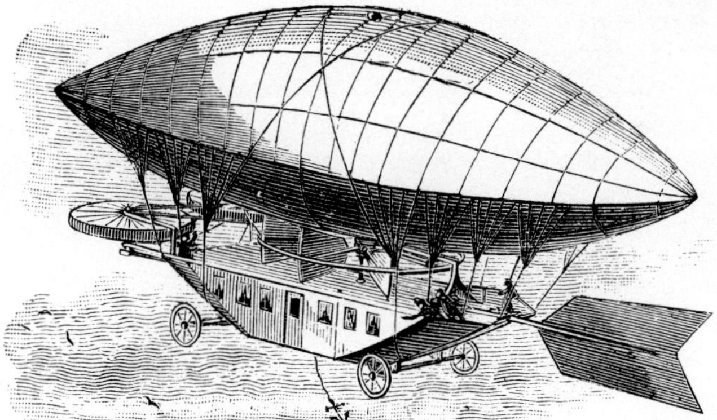
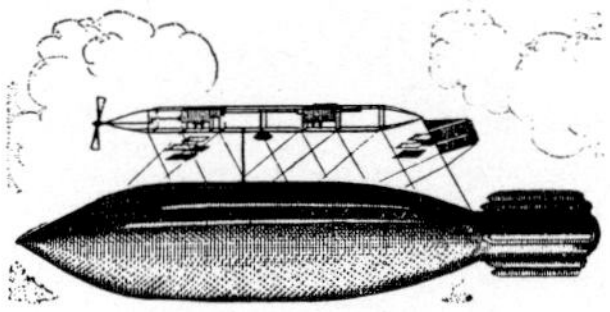

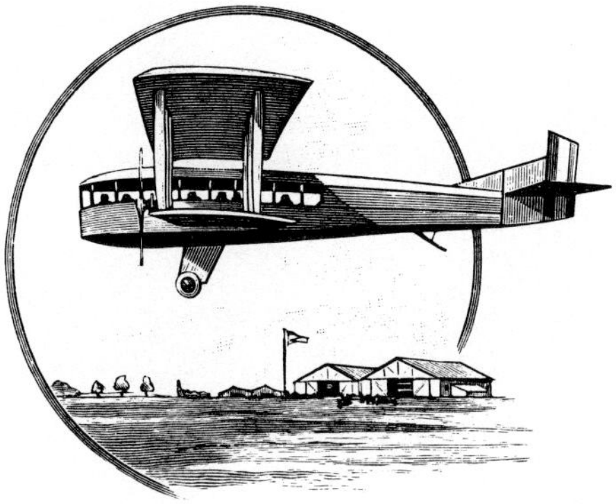

POYET

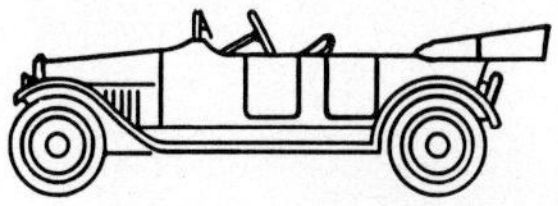

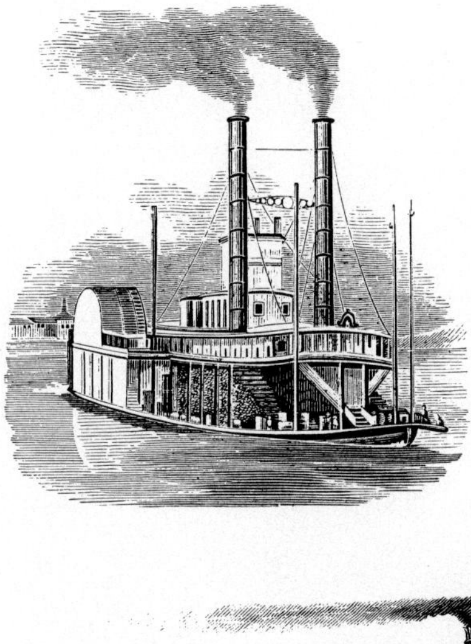

Don't Give up the Ship.

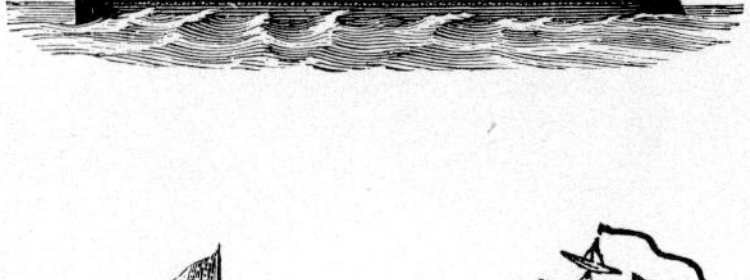

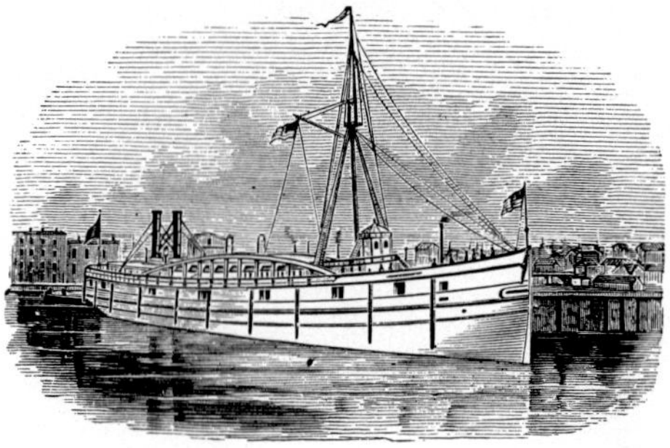

GGA
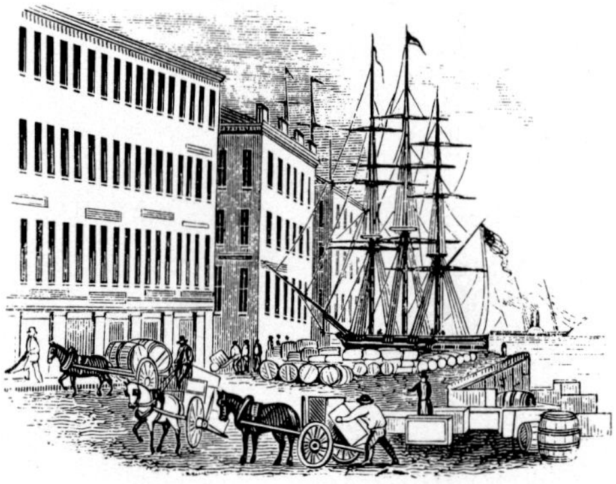

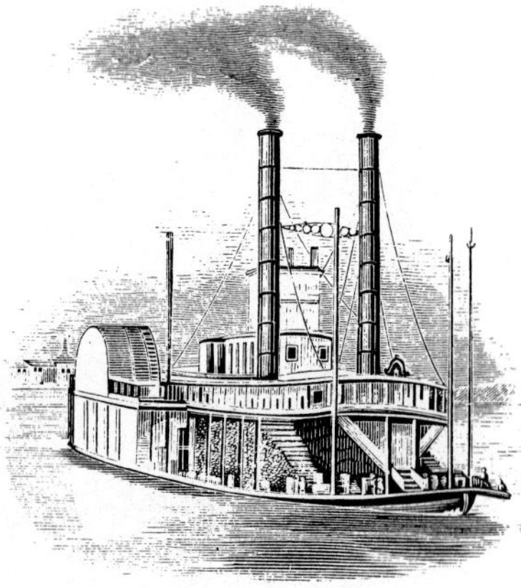

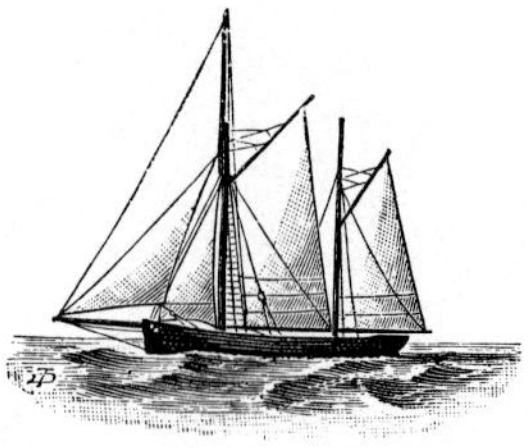

NUGENT SC